Crypto Conundrum

Money, Trust, and the Philosophy of Digital Wealth

The Curious Philosopher

Copyright Page

Disclaimer

The views and opinions expressed in this book are those of the author(s) and do not necessarily reflect the official policy or position of any other agency, organization, employer, or company. The contents of this book are for informational and educational purposes only and are not intended to serve as professional advice, diagnosis, or treatment.

The information provided in this book is believed to be accurate and reliable as of the date of publication. However, it may include some errors or inaccuracies, and no warranty or guarantee is provided regarding the accuracy, timeliness, or applicability of the content.

Readers are encouraged to consult with professional philosophers, educators, or other qualified professionals where appropriate for personalized advice. The author(s) and publisher shall not be liable for any loss, damage, or harm caused or alleged to be caused, directly or indirectly, by the

Introduction: When Money Takes a Digital Leap

Imagine a world where money isn't just coins and bills, but lines of computer code. That's the reality brought about by cryptocurrencies like Bitcoin and the technology behind them, blockchain. This isn't just some nerdy tech trend – it's a revolution with potential to reshape everything we know about how we pay for things, save, invest, and even what money truly means.

A Trip Through Money's History

For thousands of years, money has taken many forms. We've bartered with seashells, used precious metals as coins, and relied on paper backed by governments. Each step was a way of making trade and storing value easier. Then came the digital age - credit cards, online banking, and now... money that exists purely as information.

What Makes Cryptocurrencies...Different

Traditional money relies on trust in central authorities like banks and governments. Cryptocurrencies change the game. They operate on decentralized networks, sort of like a giant digital ledger shared across thousands of computers. This cuts out the middlemen, meaning transactions can potentially be faster, cheaper, and less restricted. No one person or institution owns this ledger, making crypto resistant to being shut down or manipulated.

The Potential? Huge. The Questions? Bigger.

This tech could change everything. Imagine sending money across the globe as easily as email, or micropayments that make whole new business models possible. Businesses could track their goods more efficiently with blockchain, and maybe even our voting systems could be made more secure. Crypto might even help people in countries with unstable currencies.

But it also raises major questions. Where does the value of cryptocurrency come from, if not backed by gold or governments? Can you truly trust a system designed to have no one in charge? This is why we need to go beyond just the technical aspects of cryptocurrencies, and dive into the philosophy of it all.

Thinking Like Philosophers

Philosophy means asking those big, fundamental questions. What IS money, really? What gives it value? How does money shape how we trust others and build our societies? Cryptocurrencies and digital economies force us to revisit these ancient questions in ways we never imagined.

This book is a journey into that exciting and sometimes mind-bending territory. We'll look at the implications of digital money, the ethical dilemmas it brings, and the possible futures that unfold – whether crypto transforms everything or fizzles into a footnote of history. Ready? Let's dive in...

Chapter 1: What the Heck IS Money, Anyway?

Picture this: you're at a farmer's market, and you've got your eye on a juicy tomato. Problem is, you only have a fancy painting. Tomatoes rot, paintings (mostly) don't. This is where money comes in! Economists have been pondering the exact nature of money for centuries, and they came up with a few key ideas:

Medium of Exchange: This is the most obvious part. Money is the middleman that lets you swap your painting for a tomato, or your labor for a paycheck. It avoids the whole "find-someone-who-needs-a-painting-AND-has-tomatoes" problem.

Store of Value: Money (ideally) doesn't rot like a tomato. It lets you save the value of your work or goods for later. Of course, some monies do this better than others (hello, inflation!).

Unit of Account: Think of money like a ruler for value. How many tomatoes is that painting worth? Money provides the yardstick that lets you make fair comparisons.

Where Cryptocurrencies Get Weird

Cryptocurrencies do those classic money things, but with twists:

Exchange Made Weirder: Imagine you swap your tomatoes for a special token only usable at that market. Crypto acts like that sometimes – it's exchangeable, but maybe not everywhere.

Storing Bits, Not Bills: Crypto is digital, so you're storing value in code, not a piggy bank. This can be freaky, since what if you lose your electronic 'key' to access it?

Is It Actually Scarce? Gold is valuable partly because it's rare. You can't just mine more easily. With digital stuff, it's easy to copy files. Cryptocurrencies use complex math to create artificial scarcity.

Money: It's All in Our Heads

Here's the mind-blowing bit: money only works because we all believe it works. A dollar bill has no use on its own. It's the shared belief that it represents value that makes it powerful. Cryptocurrencies take this idea to the extreme - their value rests almost entirely on belief.

So, what does this tell us?

Money is way more than coins and bills. It's an ever-evolving social agreement.

Crypto forces us to rethink what makes money valuable: scarcity, trust, and the networks it exists within.

Buckle up, because money's about to get even weirder in the digital age!

Chapter 2: Trust, But Verify... Especially in the Digital World

Imagine trusting a stranger with your life savings. Sounds crazy, right? Yet, we do a version of this with banks all the time. Traditional finance is built on trusting institutions: governments that back our money, banks that hold it, regulators who (hopefully) play fair. But what if technology could change this whole trust equation?

Banks: The Old-School Trust Middlemen

Think of banks like guarded fortresses. Your money goes in, and they promise to keep it safe and make sure only you can withdraw it. We trust them because:

Reputation: Big-name banks usually don't run away with our cash. They want to stay in business.

Regulation: Laws exist (in theory) to prevent banks from doing shady stuff.

Insurance: In some cases, if the bank fails, the government might pay you back (up to a point).

Blockchain: Doing Trust Differently

Cryptocurrencies use a technology called blockchain. Picture it as a giant, unchangeable ledger shared across thousands of computers. Each transaction, like you sending Bitcoin to a friend, is a "block" added to this chain. This offers a new kind of trust:

No Single Point of Failure: No single bank or person can mess with the ledger, making hacks or scams harder (not impossible, but harder).

Transparency: In theory, everyone can see the ledger (though who owns what can be hidden). This sunshine is its own form of accountability.

Cryptography to the Rescue: Complex math secures the system, making it super hard to fake transactions or counterfeit digital money.

The Trust Paradox

Crypto is often called "trustless". Weird, right? It means you don't need to trust a specific bank or person. Instead, you trust the technology itself and the rules baked into its code. But hold on:

Can code be perfect? Bugs and loopholes do happen, leading to lost funds.

Who makes the rules? Even decentralized systems have creators with influence.

People are messy: Scams exist even in the crypto world, preying on those who don't understand the technology.

New Trust, New Problems

Crypto shifts trust away from institutions and towards the technology itself. However, this raises new questions: Do we blindly trust code we don't fully understand? Are we swapping one set of risks (like bank failures) for different ones (like tech glitches and scams)?

The trust game has changed, and it's up to us to become smart players in this new digital landscape.

Chapter 3: The Crypto Rollercoaster – What Makes These Things Worth Anything?

One day, a Bitcoin is worth enough to buy a fancy car. The next, it might only get you a pizza. This wild ride makes understanding the value of cryptocurrencies a major headache. So, let's dig into why these digital assets are worth anything at all.

Gold vs. Crypto: A Value Tale

Intrinsic Value: Gold is shiny, useful for some things, and importantly, it's RARE. This gives it inherent value, even if you just melt it into a lump. Crypto has no inherent value. It's code, not metal.

Extrinsic Value: This comes from outside. Dollars have value because governments say so and we use them to pay taxes. Crypto's value is shakier, based on what people BELIEVE it should be worth.

Factors That Drive Crypto Value (or Hype)

Belief: If enough people believe crypto is the future, its price soars based on that belief alone.

Scarcity: Many cryptos have a limited supply baked into their code – artificial scarcity mimicking gold.

Utility: If crypto can be used for real things – payments, smart contracts – this gives it practical value.

Speculation: Let's be honest, lots of folks treat crypto like a casino chip, hoping the price goes up so they can sell. This drives wild swings.

Store of Value? That's Debatable

Can you count on crypto to hold its value like a savings account? Oof, that's the big question. Because of all the factors above, crypto prices are notoriously SWINGY. This rollercoaster ride makes it a questionable option if you need reliable purchasing power.

The Bubble Question

Some people yell "BUBBLE!" – meaning crypto prices are way higher than reasonable, driven by hype, not real value. Others say, "Nope, early days for a revolution!" This debate gets heated because, in the end, nobody truly knows for sure.

So, Worthless or the Future?

The truth is, it's too early to say. Cryptocurrencies MIGHT be transformative, or they MIGHT fizzle out. Their value ultimately depends on a few big questions:

Will people and businesses widely adopt them for real use?

Can trust and stability be improved?

Will smart regulation emerge to protect people without stifling the tech?

The answers will determine if crypto's a passing fad or a fundamental shift in how we think about value.

Chapter 4: DeFi – The Promise and the Perils

Decentralized Finance (DeFi) is a big part of the crypto buzz. It's the idea of creating a whole financial system on blockchains – loans, trading, everything – without traditional banks in the picture. This has exciting potential, but also some serious ethical questions we need to wrestle with.

The Promise: Finance for (Almost) Everyone

No Gatekeepers: Traditional banks can deny people loans based on credit score, income, etc. DeFi, in theory, could let anyone with an internet connection participate.

Global Reach: DeFi could help people in countries with unstable currencies or limited access to banking.

Creative Explosion: DeFi lets developers make new kinds of financial tools that were impossible before.

The Perils: Not All Rainbows and Unicorns

The Wild West: Many DeFi projects operate in a legal grey zone, or with no regulation at all. This makes scams and rug-pulls (where developers ditch a project and steal investor funds) a serious risk.

Technical Hurdles: DeFi can be complex. If you don't understand the code, you might make huge mistakes. This puts less tech-savvy people at a disadvantage.

Whales in the Pool: Just like in traditional finance, those with lots of money often have an unfair edge in the DeFi world.

The Energy Elephant in the Room

Some blockchains, especially Bitcoin, gobble up insane amounts of electricity. This raises huge questions:

Is it worth it?: Is the potential of DeFi worth the environmental cost?

Tech to the Rescue?: Are more sustainable blockchains emerging to address this issue?

Democratization or a New Digital Divide?

DeFi's goal is to spread financial power more evenly. Yet, if it's risky, complicated, and favors people who are already wealthy, it might create a new kind of digital inequality.

The Questions We Face

DeFi's potential is huge, but it raises significant ethical concerns:

How do we balance freedom and protection? Do we need some regulations to prevent people from getting fleeced?

Can DeFi truly be inclusive, or will it mainly benefit those with existing technical and financial advantages?

Is the environmental cost of certain blockchains justified by DeFi's potential benefits?

There are no easy answers. This is why we need to go beyond just understanding HOW DeFi works, and grapple with whether it's the kind of financial system we actually want.

Chapter 5: Crypto's Big Challenge: Can It Topple the Old Financial Order?

Cryptocurrencies aren't just about buying weird internet money; they have the potential to disrupt the entire way our economic systems function. Let's dive into how this might go down and what it could mean for everyone.

Cutting Out the Middlemen: Disinter-what-now?

"Disintermediation" is just a fancy word for removing those in-between folks. Traditionally, if you want to make a global payment, it passes through banks and other institutions. They charge fees and slow things down. Crypto offers the potential for near-instant, cheaper direct transactions, cutting these middlemen out of the picture.

The Banking Boogeyman

This sounds great, right? Well, for banks, not so much. If crypto becomes the go-to for payments, a big source of their profits could dry up. They might have to change how they do business or risk being left behind.

Hold on, Could Crypto Replace My Dollars?

This is the trillion-dollar question (literally). Right now, most of us get paid, pay bills, and save in government-backed currencies, called "fiat" money. Crypto's wild price swings make that impractical for most folks. But could that change?

The Stability Factor: If cryptos become less volatile, they become more viable as actual everyday currencies.

The Trust Factor: People generally trust their government's money (even if they grumble about it). Crypto needs to overcome a trust hurdle.

Governments Get in the Crypto Game

Plot twist! Central banks, the folks who MAKE fiat money, are developing their OWN digital currencies, or CBDCs. These could offer some of crypto's benefits (fast transfers) while maintaining government control. Think of it as the establishment striking back.

Hedge Against Trouble?

Some folks hope crypto can be a shield against bad financial times:

Inflation Buster?: If government prints too much money, prices soar (inflation). Crypto's limited supply, in theory, makes it inflation-resistant

Safe Harbor: Maybe in countries with unstable currencies, crypto offers a more reliable store of value. But remember, crypto is volatile too!

Revolution or Side Show?

The big question is whether cryptocurrencies will fundamentally transform how money and financial systems work, or stay a niche for investment and tech experimentation. The answer depends on factors like:

Will user-friendly crypto products make it accessible to the average person?

Can crypto gain enough trust to be widely adopted?

Will governments embrace, regulate, or try to squash crypto?

This chapter has no ending, because the story is still being written!

Chapter 6: Beyond the Buck: Crypto's Makeover of Our World

So far, we've focused on crypto as a new kind of money. But the tech behind it has the potential to sneak into nearly every aspect of our lives. Think of it as the early days of the internet – we started with clunky email, and now we have it powering everything from shopping to dating.

Crypto's Toolkit: Why It's More Than Cash

The Unfakeable Record: Blockchains create a record that's tough to change. Imagine tracking the journey of a medicine bottle for safety, luxury goods to verify they aren't knock-offs, or even votes to ensure they haven't been tampered with.

Digital You: Crypto can provide secure digital identities, giving you control over your data instead of big tech companies. This could change how we log in to websites, prove our credentials, etc.

Smart Contracts: Picture tiny computer programs on the blockchain. These could automate all sorts of agreements, potentially cutting out lawyers for simple stuff.

Roadblock Ahead: Rules of the Game

Innovation is great, but unregulated innovation risks scams and chaos. Governments are grappling with how to handle crypto:

Protecting the People: How do you stop crypto fraud when the criminals could be anywhere in the world?

Taxes!: Governments kinda like collecting taxes. They need ways to make sure folks pay what's owed on crypto gains.

Balancing Freedom & Control: The whole point of crypto is decentralization. Too much regulation could kill the good parts along with the bad.

Crystal Ball Time: What Kind of Future?

Here's a few scenarios to get your imagination going:

Crypto Niche: It stays a thing for investors and tech nerds, but mainstream folks stick to dollars.

Hybrid World: Crypto becomes ONE part of our financial system, alongside traditional money and CBDCs.

Crypto Takeover: Maybe way in the future, most of our transactions and important records live on blockchains. Wild!

Is Adoption Inevitable?

That depends on a few things:

User-friendliness: Can crypto be made as easy to use as your banking app?

Stability: If prices keep doing crazy dances, it'll turn off regular people.

The Narrative: Does crypto win the trust of the public and overcome its negative image?

This chapter doesn't have easy answers, but asks exciting questions. The potential is wild, the obstacles are real, and the ultimate shape of our crypto-flavored future depends on the choices we make right now!

Conclusion: Money Gets a Mind-Bending Upgrade

Throughout this book, we've journeyed into the weird and wonderful world of cryptocurrencies and digital economies. We've seen how these technologies challenge age-old beliefs about money, trust, and the way our economic systems are built.

The Big Philosophical Takeaways

Money is...a shared story? The value of anything, whether gold or a Bitcoin, comes down to collective belief. Crypto forces us to see this more clearly than ever.

Trust isn't just about people anymore: Crypto makes us rethink trust. Can we trust code and mathematical systems as much as (or even more than) human institutions?

Power Shifts: Decentralization promises to redistribute financial power. But will it actually make things fairer, or create new imbalances?

Crypto's Place in Money's Long History

For thousands of years, the form of money constantly evolved. Cryptocurrencies are a major leap, perhaps as big as the shift from metal coins to paper. But will they become the dominant way we exchange value, or settle into a niche role?

An Ever-Changing Landscape

The one thing we know for sure is that technology will continue to mess with our economic realities. This is why we desperately need continued philosophical analysis alongside technological advancement. We must ask ourselves:

What kind of financial systems do we want? Ones built on trust in institutions, or in code?

How should the benefits and risks of crypto innovation be distributed fairly?

Can we design technology that serves society's needs, rather than letting the tech dictate what society becomes?

The Adventure Isn't Over

This book hasn't provided all the answers. In a way, it can't. The story of crypto and digital economies is being written in real-time. The choices we make, the debates we have, and the way we regulate (or don't regulate) these technologies will shape the kind of future we inhabit.

This calls for everyone – not just techies or investors – to become educated, engage in the discussion, and demand that the evolution of money works to the benefit of all.

About The Curious Philosopher

Welcome to The Curious Philosopher, your dedicated platform for diving deep into the world of philosophy. We are more than just a YouTube channel or a book publisher. We are a beacon of enlightenment, making complex philosophical concepts accessible and engaging for all.

Our YouTube channel is a rich repository of philosophy made simple. We take the profound and often complex ideas from the world of philosophy and break them down into digestible, easy-to-understand content. From the ancient wisdom of Socrates to the existentialist thoughts of Sartre, we cover a broad spectrum of philosophical schools and thoughts, making philosophy accessible to everyone, regardless of their background or prior knowledge.

As a book publisher, we take the same approach, transforming intricate philosophical theories into comprehensible narratives. Our books are not just collections of words, but vessels of wisdom that make philosophy approachable and relatable. We believe that philosophy should not be confined to academic circles, but should be available to all who seek to understand the world and their place in it.

At The Curious Philosopher, we believe in the power of curiosity and the pursuit of knowledge. We are here to stoke the fires of your curiosity, to guide you on your intellectual journey, and to help you navigate the fascinating world of philosophy.

If you are someone who is not afraid to question, to explore, and to learn, then you are in the right place. Join us on this journey of exploration, as we make philosophy easy to understand, one concept at a time.

Be sure to visit our Youtube channel at:

https://www.curiousphilosopher.com/youtube

You can also visit us on the web at

https://www.curiousphilosopher.com

Welcome to The Curious Philosopher. Stay curious. Stay enlightened.

www.ingramcontent.com/pod-product-compliance
Lightning Source LLC
Chambersburg PA
CBHW070456290526
45791CB00005B/2138